When my mind fills with dark thoughts,
I will put my trust in God.

When my faith is small,
I will put my trust in God.

When to simply trust
is the hardest thing of all,
I will put my trust in God.

For

_____

From

_____

When I'm Alone

Thoughts and Prayers That Comfort

Ron DelBene

WITH

Mary & Herb Montgomery

The Upper Room

NASHVILLE, TENNESSEE

WHEN I'M ALONE

This booklet is part of a series of resources which also includes: *Into The Light: A Simple Way to Pray with the Sick and the Dying*, *Near Life's End: What Family and Friends Can Do*, and *A Time to Mourn: Recovering from the Death of a Loved One*.

Scripture quotations not otherwise identified are from the Revised Standard Version of the Bible, copyrighted 1946, 1952, and © 1971 by the Division of Christian Education, National Council of the Churches of Christ in the United States of America, and are used by permission.

Scripture quotations designated KJV are from the King James Version of the Bible.

An abbreviated version of "Morning Prayers" reprinted with permission of SCM Press (London) and of Macmillan Publishing Company from LETTERS AND PAPERS FROM PRISON, Enlarged Edition by Dietrich Bonhoeffer copyright © 1967, 1971 by SCM Press Ltd.

Epigraph from JUSTICE AND MERCY by Reinhold Niebuhr. Copyright © 1974 by Ursula Niebuhr. Reprinted by permission of Harper & Row Publishers, Inc.

Selected lines from MARKINGS by Dag Hammarskjold translated by W. H. Auden and Leif Sjoberg, © 1964 by Alfred A. Knopf, Inc. and Faber and Faber, Ltd., Used by permission of Alfred A. Knopf, Inc. and Faber and Faber Ltd.

All black and white photographs are by Herb Montgomery.

Cover Transparency: Robert E. Gantner
Cover and Book Design: Jim Bateman
First Printing: March, 1988 (10)
Second Printing: March, 1989 (10)
ISBN 0-8358-0579-4

Printed in the United States of America

Contents

The Prayer Within

When we're alone, sick, and uncertain about tomorrow, we may find that traditional prayers aren't as satisfying as they once were. Thoughts wander. Medication may dull the mind. Pain might make it hard to focus. We may feel that God is distant and not much concerned about us. Perhaps we have prayed for a healing and gotten nothing but bad news from nurses and doctors.

Will anything help? In the midst of distress and discouragement isn't there something that will comfort in long, lonely hours? something that will focus the mind? something that will keep us in closer touch with God?

Many of us who have asked these questions have found the breath prayer to be that special "something." This prayer is nothing we are taught. Rather it is one we discover for ourselves. It lies within us like a tiny seed that, when nurtured, will grow and flower into a new closeness with God. Perhaps the person who gave you this booklet has already helped you discover your prayer. Here are the five easy steps to follow. If reading is difficult, ask someone to read the steps to you.

Step One

Sit or lie in as comfortable a position as possible. Then be calm and quiet. Close your eyes and remind yourself that God loves you and that you are in God's presence. Recall a favorite passage from scripture that places you in a restful frame of mind. "Be still, and know that I am God" (Psalm 46:10) is a line people often find helpful.

7

Step Two

As you keep your eyes closed, imagine that God is calling you by name. Listen carefully and hear God asking you: "(*Your name*), what do you want?"

Step Three

Answer God with whatever comes honestly from your heart. Your answer may be a single word, such as *peace* or *love* or *forgiveness*. Your answer may instead be a phrase or brief sentence, such as "I want to feel your forgiveness" or "I want to understand your love" or "I want to be with you." Whatever your response is, it becomes the heart of your prayer.

Step Four

Choose your favorite name for God. (Choices people commonly make include God, Jesus, Christ, Lord, Spirit, Shepherd, Creator.)

Step Five

Combine your name for God with your answer to God's question "What do you want?" and you have your prayer. For example:

What I Want	Name I call God	Possible Prayer
peace	God	Let me know your peace, O God.
love	Jesus	Jesus, let me feel your love.
rest	Shepherd	My Shepherd, let me rest in thee.

What do you do if several ideas occur? You need to eliminate or combine ideas until you have focused your prayer. You may "want" many things. But if you think carefully, you can narrow your wants to a specific need that you feel is as basic to your spiritual well-being as water is to life. Thus the question you need to ask yourself is: What do I want that will make me feel most whole? Once you achieve a feeling of wholeness, peace of mind and heart will follow.

When you have gotten to the core of your needs, search for words that give it expression. Then work with the words until you have a prayer of six to eight syllables. The words should flow smoothly whether spoken aloud or expressed silently as heart-thoughts.

Your prayer may be most rhythmic when God's name is placed at the beginning, but try it at the end as well. One way will feel better than another. When your prayer seems right for you, write it down. Then use if often throughout the day. Whenever you think of it, repeat the prayer several times. You can whisper it. You can say it aloud. You can think it. In time, your breath prayer will become as natural as breathing. Even when you are not consciously praying, the words will play in your heart like a refrain from a favorite song.

This is my breath prayer:

_____

"I Am with You Always"

There often comes a time when we get so sick of being sick that we look for anything that might help us focus on something other than illness. This is a time when the breath prayer can be especially comforting.

How can prayer—any prayer—bring order and a measure of comfort out of the chaos that often accompanies illness? To pray is to raise the mind and heart to God, to respond to our God who promises, "I am with you always" (Matt. 28:20). The promise has special meaning when we are sick. It says to us that we will never be alone with our anxiety or fear or suffering. Through it all, God is with us. And it is through prayer that we are most likely to feel God's caring, comforting presence.

The breath prayer helps us feel God's presence in a special way. This ancient way of praying takes its name from the Hebrew word _ruach_, which can be translated as "wind," "breath," or "spirit." It is the _ruach_ of God that is breathed into all living beings. Because this way of praying reminds us that we share God's breath, and because the prayer can come as easily and naturally as breathing, it is known as the breath prayer.

The breath prayer can be said effortlessly at any time or place. Through its use we are thus better able to follow the apostle Paul's call to "pray without ceasing" (1 Thess. 5:17, KJV).

There are many ways to pray, and the breath prayer is just one of them. This personal prayer that arises from within us is a way to unite and unify all the other ways we pray. Although the breath prayer is individualized and very personal, much of its effectiveness comes from sharing it

11

with others. When those who love and care about us use our prayer, it puts on their lips what is in our heart. It enables them to pray not just *for* us but *with* us.

In this book you will find other thoughts and prayers meant to help during times of distress. I trust that some of them will speak to your heart. Read the prayers (or ask someone to read them to you) as a source of comfort and spiritual nourishment. Remember that when you are steadfast in prayer—no matter what the prayer may be— you grow in your awareness of God's presence. And God, who has promised to be with you always, will sustain and strengthen you in whatever trials you face.

A Psalm of David

Although we may at times feel out of touch with God, God is never out of touch with us. God is the Good Shepherd who never deserts us, the Shepherd who will see us through the darkest of valleys and whose love and care for us are everlasting.

> The LORD is my shepherd;
> I shall not want.
> He maketh me to lie down in green pastures:
> he leadeth me beside the still waters.
> He restoreth my soul:
> he leadeth me in the paths of righteousness
> for his name's sake.
> Yea, though I walk through the valley
> of the shadow of death,
> I will fear no evil:
> for thou art with me;
> thy rod and thy staff they comfort me.
> Thou preparest a table before me
> in the presence of mine enemies:
> thou anointest my head with oil;
> my cup runneth over.
> Surely goodness and mercy shall follow me
> all the days of my life:
> and I will dwell in the house of the LORD for ever.
> Amen.

—Psalm 23, KJV

Whatever This Day Brings

We are all part of a suffering world. Whatever our sorrows, they have been felt by others. So, too, has our pain. While a man awaited execution in a Nazi prison during World War II, he expressed his anguish in a prayer. The words speak for all of us when our burdens become too heavy to carry alone.

O God, early in the morning I cry to you.
Help me to pray
And to concentrate my thoughts on you:
I cannot do this alone.
In me there is darkness,
But with you there is light;
I am lonely, but you do not leave me;
I am feeble in heart, but with you there is help;
I am restless, but with you there is peace.
In me there is bitterness, but with you there is patience;
I do not understand your ways,
But you know the way for me. . . .

Restore me to liberty,
And enable me so to live now
That I may answer before you and before men.
Lord, whatever this day may bring,
Your name be praised.

—Dietrich Bonhoeffer

Personal Prayers

We each have our own way of talking to God, but sometimes what is in our heart needs help in finding its way to our lips. The prayers included here express anxieties and speak of yearnings we may feel. Such prayers are but starting points for our own. They encourage us to turn to God and express our innermost thoughts and deepest needs.

When I'm Afraid

God, I have fears I cannot handle alone.
I fear for my fate and for that of my family.
I fear for the trials I face today
and the uncertainties of tomorrow.
So, like a child turning to a parent, I come to you
and ask that I might feel your comforting presence.
I believe that with you all things are possible.
With your help, I will be able to face my fears
and accept whatever lies ahead for me. Amen.

When I'm Weary

I want to be thankful for the life
you have given me, Lord.
But lately I find it hard to face another day.
The hours drag by. My body has no energy.
I cannot remember what it was like to feel well.
I am so weary, God. So very weary.
I come to you asking for strength.
I place myself in your hands
and trust that you will hold me
in your protective love. Amen.

When I'm Discouraged

Another day is passing.
I find it hard to eat. I find it hard to sleep.
I am so discouraged.
I feel my energy slipping away and
am helpless to do anything about it.
And yet, God, something good happens as I talk
honestly with you.
In the midst of discouragement,
you and I are close.
I thank you for that warm awareness
that lets me know I am not alone.
I pray that others who feel discouraged
may sense that closeness just as I do. Amen.

When I'm in Pain

God, you know there are days when my pain
is like a cloud that blocks the sun
and prevents me from seeing
a bright side to anything.
Was I short-tempered today?
Mean-spirited?
Hurtful to anyone?
If so, I am sorry.
Help anyone I offended to understand
that I don't want to be difficult.
Please grant me the strength to bear my pain.
Please give me a restful, peace-filled hour.
I pray in Jesus' name. Amen.

When I'm Lonely

I get so very lonely, Lord.
Once I was able to go out to where people are.
Now I have to wait for them to come to me.
Help me guard against morbid thoughts
that lead to self-pity.
Guide me instead to recall pleasant memories
and to think on those things that
speak of life's goodness.
When friends and family come to visit,
prevent me from boring them
with complaints and details of my ills.
Instead, grant me the grace to share with them
those kind thoughts and loving memories
that bind us together.
I ask this in Jesus' name. Amen.

When the End Seems Near

I have enjoyed this world you created, God,
and I hope to see yet another dawn.
But if this should be
my last day of earthly life,
I pray especially for those who have loved me
and for those who will mourn my passing.
I believe that the ending of this life
is but the beginning of a new life with you:
a new life in a place of peace and love that
is beyond anything I can imagine.
I thank you, God, for all my blessings
and ask that your will be done. Amen.

When I Seek Forgiveness

Dear God, my heart is troubled
and I yearn to feel at peace.
There are things in my life for which I am sorry.
There are the cruel words
that should have gone unspoken;
the good I could have done and did not do;
the love I should have given
that went unexpressed;
the times I turned away from you
by breaking your commandments.
Please know that I am sorry
for the wrongs I have committed and
for my failures to love and care about others
as you have called me to do.
I seek your forgiveness, God,
and ask also that you grant me the grace
to forgive myself. Amen.

When Evening Comes

As the light of this day ends
and the darkness of night descends,
I reflect on times gone by.
In my life there have been peaks of joy
as well as valleys of hurt and discouragement.
Through it all, God, I have been glad
that you gave me life.
Please give special strength
to those who worry about me.
Help them to be thankful for their lives
as I am thankful for mine.
Bless others who are suffering
and lead us all to a place of peace. Amen.

Gifts We Can Give

No matter what our circumstance, no matter how ill or incapacitated we may be, we are still able to do some things. We can still be loving; we can still be forgiving; and these are the greatest gifts we can give one another. Through love and forgiveness, we bring light to dark places and heal the bruised spots in relationships with friends and family. With love and forgiveness, we become instruments of God's peace, a peace "which passes all understanding" (Phil. 4:7).

Lord, make me an instrument of your peace.
Where there is hatred, let me sow love,
Where there is injury, pardon;
Where there is doubt, faith;
Where there is despair, hope;
Where there is darkness, light;
Where there is sadness, joy.

O divine Master, grant that I may not so much seek
To be consoled, as to console,
To be understood, as to understand,
To be loved, as to love,
For it is in giving that we receive;
It is in pardoning that we are pardoned;
It is in dying that we are born to eternal life.

—Francis of Assisi

A Different Answer

Each of us can remember times when we asked for something in prayer and did not feel that God answered. A prayer believed to have been written by a Confederate soldier during the Civil War shows us that blessings can be found in outcomes we did not seek.

I asked for strength
  that I might achieve,

I was made weak
  that I might learn humbly to obey.

I asked for health
  that I might do greater things,

I was given infirmity
  that I might do better things.

I asked for riches
  that I might be happy;

I was given poverty
  that I might be wise.

I asked for power
  that I might have the praise of men;

I was given weakness
  that I might feel the need of God.

I asked for all things
  that I might enjoy life;

I was given life
that I might enjoy all things.

I got nothing that I had asked for—
but everything that I had hoped for.

Almost despite myself,
my unspoken prayers were answered;

I am . . . most richly blessed.

—Unknown Confederate Soldier

_ O God, Our Help, Our Hope _

An old hymn speaks of the comfort that comes from God's abiding presence. As we read the words to the hymn, the familiar melody plays in the mind and sings in the heart.

O God, our help in ages past, our hope for years to come, our shelter from the stormy blast, and our eternal home:

under the shadow of thy throne thy saints have dwelt secure; sufficient is thine arm alone, and our defense is sure.

Before the hills in order stood, or earth received her frame, from everlasting thou art God, to endless years the same.

A thousand ages in thy sight are like an evening gone; short as the watch that ends the night before the rising sun.

Time, like an ever rolling stream, bears all our years away; they fly, forgotten, as a dream dies at the opening day.

O God, our help in ages past, our hope for years to come, be thou our guide while life shall last, and our eternal home.

—Isaac Watts

Thoughts to Reflect Upon

I learned that it is possible for us to create
light and sound and order within us, no matter
what calamity may befall us in the outer world.
> —Helen Keller

I am serene because I know thou lovest me.
Because thou lovest me,
naught can move me from my peace.
Because thou lovest me,
I am as one to whom all good has come.
> —Translated from Gaelic by Alistair MacLean

At some moment I did answer Yes to Someone—or
Something—and from that hour I was certain that
existence is meaningful and that, therefore, my
life in self-surrender, had a goal. From that
moment I have known what it means "not to look
back" and "to take no thought for the morrow."
> —Dag Hammarskjold

God, give us grace to accept with serenity the
things that cannot be changed, courage to change
the things that should be changed, and the wisdom
to distinguish the one from the other.
> —Reinhold Niebuhr

Let not your hearts be troubled; believe in God, believe also in me. In my Father's house are many rooms; if it were not so, would I have told you that I go to prepare a place for you? And when I go and prepare a place for you, I will come again and will take you to myself, that where I am you may be also.

—John 14:1–3

I am the resurrection,
and the life.
Those who believe in me,
though they die,
yet shall they live forever,
and whoever lives and believes in me
shall never die.

—John 11:25-26, adpt.

Ron DelBene holds a master's degree in theology from Marquette University and has done additional post-graduate work in education, psychology, and counseling. He has been an assistant professor of theology, director of a campus ministry center, and National Consultant in Religion for an education division of CBS. Since 1963, Ron has been conducting programs in the area of religion—integrating educational, psychological, and therapeutic approaches to growth and development with religious experiences.

Grounded in his parish ministry experience, Ron presently leads retreats and conferences on prayer and spiritual direction. He is an Advisory Board Member and Faculty of the National Academy for Spiritual Formation sponsored by the United Methodist Church. He has worked with various denominational judicatories in retreat and spiritual formation work, as well as Cursillo, Walk to Emmaus, and Kairos (a prison ministry).

Ron is an Episcopal priest and the Missioner for Spiritual Development for the Diocese of Alabama. With his wife, Eleanor, he directs The Hermitage, a place for people to enter into solitude and prayer under their direction. He has published numerous articles and is also author of *The Breath of Life*, *Hunger of the Heart*, and *Alone with God*.

Ron and Eleanor and their two children, Paul and Anne, live in Trussville, Alabama.